# THE REAL FACE OF ILLUMINATI: TRUTH AND MYTHS ABOUT THE SECRET

Society Shrouded in Mystery – Illuminati Secrets Revealed!

**BERNADINE CHRISTNER**

# TABLE OF CONTENTS

# INTRODUCTION

This book includes valuable information on the Illuminati, including its history, aims, beliefs, and several well-known conspiracy theories related to the group.

The Order of the Illuminati and other secret organizations have often been the subject of heated arguments over their role in human history. The number of individuals who believe the Illuminati secretly control the globe or a hoax has climbed. The facts concerning the Illuminati have been distorted into falsehoods and myths, making it impossible to do an independent study on the Order.

In general, the word Illuminati refers to an elite organization that is claimed to rule the globe. Although some people understand the meaning of the name, many people, groups, and sects are confused about the Order's relationship with Freemasonry, its aims, activities, beliefs, and secrecy.

The hunt for the truth about the Order of the Illuminati is generally always a difficult endeavor. This is because most websites that provide knowledge on the Order either deny or ridicule anything related to the Illuminati. Some websites even substantiate material or data that is based only on myths and hearsay. In any case, many scholars end up with a distorted view of the Order of the Illuminati.

As a result, obtaining a truth regarding the Illuminati Order may be difficult, considering its history is often rewritten and even changed by those in power. Furthermore, like any other secret organization, the Illuminati Order is meant to be kept hidden.

This book seeks to construct a more accurate image of the Illuminati Order based on verifiable evidence, much of which is written and accounted for by certain Secret Societies initiates.

# CHAPTER 1
# THE ILLUMINATI'S EARLY BEGINNINGS

There have been many various things mentioned about the Illuminati; there have also been numerous myths and hypotheses added to its notoriety in current times. They have been described as one of the world's most powerful secret organizations, the ones pulling strings and enacting important events that have a big impact on humanity, all in a drive for global dominance. Is this, however, the case? Are the Illuminati indeed the terrible cloaked individuals that they are often depicted to be?

Let's start with the classic Illuminati hierarchy.

According to available sources, Adam Weishaupt, a Practical Philosophy and Canon Law professor at the University of Ingolstadt, established the Bavarian Illuminati (also known as the Ancient Illuminated Seers of Bavaria) on May 1st, 1776. Pope Clement XIV ordered the Society of Jesus (the Jesuits) a few years before his position at the institution. As a result, Jesuits were forced to resign from their posts at the institutions they created. In reality, Weishaupt was schooled by the same group when he was younger.

When Weishaupt was appointed to the university post, both hostile and favorable Jesuits were very contentious. There are also various accounts concerning his stay there. Some claim he was antagonistic to both the Jesuits and the Catholic Church. However, some tales speak of his negative encounters with ex-Jesuits who remained at the institution and were not interested in the more liberal courses.

That was being taught at the time. Many consider the latter to be the trigger, the cause for Weishaupt's founding of the Illuminati.

The Bavarian order's mission was to rid the people's minds of superstition and bigotry. They urged people to be kind and taught them that doing so is the way to happiness. Keep in mind that Bavaria was fiercely Catholic at the time, and people's dread of superstition was undoubtedly pervasive. They were strongly opposed to the influence of religion in people's everyday lives, as well as abuses of governmental authority. Many individuals shared the same values, yet the order's membership increased slowly.

There were just five members when it was created. Weishaupt, as well as four law students, Massenhausen, Merz, Bauhof, and Sutor. During their meetings, all five adopted identities and were known inside the order as Spartacus, Ajax, Tiberius, Agathon, and Erasmus Roterodamus. Sutor was expelled from the order for laziness.

Massenhausen led the group's recruitment and growth, bringing in Xavier von Zwack, a former pupil of Weishaupt's. Following this, a sequence of events occurred, and Masshenhausen severed connections with the order. Zwack had taken charge of the order's Munich group at this point, and the total membership had climbed to twelve. Despite Zwack's efforts, the order's membership growth remained modest. Baron Adolphe Francois Frederic Knigge (alias: Philo) joined the group in 1780. Along with him came the rituals for three degrees of symbolic Freemasonry and ten more employed inside the Illuminati. From 1780 to 1783, the Illuminati rose from a dozen to nearly 3,000 members.

There is a lot of power when there are many people, which the government did not miss. By late 1783, rumors were growing that the Illuminati group planned to overthrow the government and impose their own beliefs on the country. Duke Karl Theodor, the Elector Palatinate of Bavaria at the time, started to issue Edicts ordering the destruction of the Illuminati, fearing the end of his rule. The first was sent on June 22, 1784, and it was repeated three times in 1785. After these Edicts were issued, being linked with the Illuminati became dangerous for members in Bavaria.

Of course, there were implications for its originator as well. In 1785, Weishaupt was fired from his University position and expelled from Bavaria. He was given a pension but turned it down. Duke Ernst II of SachsenGothaAlternburg, Thuringia, Germany, granted him shelter and a position at the University of Gottingen. He spent the remainder of his years as a professor there until his death on November 18, 1830.

## The Following Years:

Information about the order's objectives and ceremonies was gathered from papers released by Weishaupt beginning in 1785. Others were retrieved by examining all the letters and documents discovered at Xavier von Zwack's home. This search yielded at least 200 separate letters, including interactions between Weishaupt and the other Illuminati leaders. There are instances like this.

There is substantial controversy over the Zwack records, with some claiming that they were not intended for the general public but rather for the state itself. After the fact, it was in the late 1700s that the government became particularly hostile to secret organizations. They were endangered, particularly by organizations with strong and wealthy men, such as the Illuminati.

It should come as no surprise that membership in the Bavarian Illuminati plummeted after the 1784 Edicts. They did, however, leave a legacy of writing and inspired a plethora of novels to be written on them. Authors who were antagonistic to the Illuminati and Masonry initially published their reviews of the secret organizations, many of which were harsh and inaccurate. Even the Masons issued material criticizing the Bavarian Illuminati, claiming that the organization merited little more than a footnote in history.

This, however, was not to be the case.

# CHAPTER 2
# THE ILLUMINATI'S RELIGIOUS BACKGROUND

The Illuminati believe Moses and other biblical figures are images of Egyptian Pharaohs. According to them, the Jewish genealogy starts with Abraham, who married his sister Sarah and then proceeded to Egypt to conquer and slay Amenmhet I (12th Dynasty). He was, after that, known as Pharaoh Amenemhet I, the first Pharaoh of unknown origin and without royal lineage. Because Sarah was unable to conceive, Moses subsequently married a second wife, an Egyptian called Hager. When she did, and Isaac was born, Abraham said that God told him to sacrifice him but afterward regretted it. When Abraham died, his body was placed in the Ark of the Covenant.

Isaac, his son, had two twin sons called Jacob and Esau. And because of their conflicts, Jacob escaped to what is now known as Israel, only to return years later with his twelve sons and tribe (the Hyksos) to topple the Egyptian Pharaoh. He crowned himself King Jakubher after his victory. However, Egyptian people revolted and drove them to the higher portions of Egypt with two monarchs from the local Egyptian dynasty in the south. Ahmose I, Kamose's brother, staged a victorious uprising against the Hyksos, driving them totally out of Egypt. As a result, Ahmose I was the first monarch of the 18th dynasty, and he founded a new kingdom based on a military empire.

The Hyksos returned to Canaan and divided the territory into twelve states, each of which belonged to one of the twelve sons and was named after them. On the other hand, Joseph remained in Egypt and concealed his Hebrew origins by marrying an Egyptian lady called Asenath, daughter of Poliphera, priest of On. He received his dream interpreting abilities. He then changed his name to Zaphnath Paaneah (Imhotep), becoming the greatest official and eventually the top priest during the reign of Pharaoh Djoser (Ahmose I Aka.

Pharaoh Netjerikhet, Pharaoh of the 3rd dynasty, 2670 BC in lower Egypt). Jacob ascended to power by deftly reading the Pharaoh's dreams. Then, as Pharaoh vizor and chief-priest, he governed Egypt and purchased Egyptian land from the hungry people for the Pharaoh. He taxed them on their revenue, and under his leadership, the Hebrews returned to Egypt, were protected, and thrived, reaching a population of two million by the time of the Exodus.

Moses was born three hundred years after Joseph's reign, during the reign of Thutmose I (the third Pharaoh of the XVIII dynasty, 1503-1493BC). Thutmose had five boys, including a daughter called Hatshepsut and a son called Thutmose II, who married her later in life. However, since Hatshepsut could not give an heir to the throne, Thutmose II had a son with a non-royal mistress named Isis, named Thutmose III (the Biblical Moses) reared him as her son. Moses (Thutmose III, 1479-1425) became Pharaoh of Egypt and led campaigns against the Hyksos in Canaan, eventually conquering it in 1406BC.

Pharaoh Psusennes II, often known as King David, became the king of Israel in 1003 BC. In 970 BC, his son, Pharaoh Siamun, commonly known as the legendary King Solomon, ascended to the throne. Solomon's temple became a center for the worship of gold animals and orgies and the sacrifice of women and children. The tales about Amun and depictions of this God as jealous, racial, greedy, furious, and vindictive are similar to those surrounding Abraham's God. The word Amen, which Christians, Muslims, Hindus, and Jews use after a prayer, alludes to the Egyptian God Amun-Ra, ruler of evil and chaos, and signifies "the hidden one." The Amun sign may be seen in numerous locations across the globe, including the Vatican City.

# CHAPTER 3

# THE ORDER'S THREE GRADES

The three levels of the Order of the Illuminati are described briefly below:

## Bavarian beginner

Members of the Illuminati are claimed to be lured and introduced to the Order via enticing language about the pursuit of enlightenment, wisdom, and esoteric knowledge. Novice Illuminati members were also exposed to a constantly monitored hierarchy and control, similar to the structure utilized by the Jesuits. The Order's political aims are not addressed in this grade.

Scholars and historians agree that once a novice is enrolled, the training is in the hands of the enroller. The enroller conceals the identities of the remainder of the superiors from the novice. Throughout the novitiate phase, the Order's goal is to enhance and perfect the novice's moral character, pique his interest in admirable aspects that obstruct the activities and methods of bad persons, broaden his human and social ideas, and assist good persons in finding good positions in the world.

Furthermore, the novice is impressed with the obligation to preserve total confidentiality and respect the Order's business throughout the novitiate term. Following that, the novice will be forced to control his egotistic desires and viewpoints while maintaining complete obedience and respect for his superiors.

A complete report on oneself is one of the most important aspects of a novice's responsibilities. This will be kept in the Order's archives. The report should contain detailed information on the novice's family and personal career. It should also contain distant elements such as the names of the novice's adversaries and the incidence of the hostility, titles of books he has, his strong and weak character traits, the names of his parents, siblings, and relatives, and his parents' dominating interests, among other things. The novice must also submit monthly reports detailing the advantages of the Order and his provided services.

To rise to the higher grades, the novice must stay a novitiate for about two years and serve in the recruiting job. His performance and success in recruitment will determine his progress. When the novice recruits and enrolls another novice, he becomes the latter's superior. Once the superiors have determined that the novice is deserving of progress, he will be inducted to the Minerval grade or degree.

## Minerval

Minerval is derived from Minerva, the Roman goddess of poetry, knowledge, weaving, healing, trade, magic, crafts, and music. Minerva is often connected with an owl, which is regarded to be her holy creature. The owl, on the other hand, is revered for its wise advice. Minerva is commonly featured as an ancient emblem of the mysteries in various locations, including the Great Seal of California and the Library of Congress.

Indoctrination is part of the Order's second grade or degree. In this grade, initiates are educated about the Order's spiritual ideals; yet, they still do not have enough knowledge about Weishaupt and his close administrators' true intentions or purposes.

In the Minerval grade, initiates are required to be rid of any residual doubts regarding the Order's ultimate goal: to bring down the wealthy and powerful or topple governmental institutions and religious organizations. During the initiation ritual, the initiate swears to be of service to humanity, obey all superiors and the Order's regulations, preserve total silence and loyalty, and sacrifice all personal interests for the sake of society.

One of the minervals' advantages is the opportunity to meet a handful of their superiors, known as the Illuminated Minervals. Minervals might get engaged in conversations with their superiors, which may be a wonderful source of inspiration for them.

## Minerval Illuminated

Only a small number of Minervals rise to the level of Illuminated Minerval. In this grade, the erstwhile novice and initiate become superiors and are assigned duties to prepare them to operate in the actual world. The majority of the Illuminated Minerval members' work focuses on studying humanity and the refinement of methodology.

Each Illuminated Minerval member is given a small group of Minervals to examine and lead in a certain path. As a result, the Order's lower-level members serve as test subjects for procedures and procedures applied to the masses in general.

Mastery in the skill of leading or directing men is required for the grade 'Illuminated Minerval.' To be the director of men's consciences and become skilled psychologists, members must keep track of their acts and continually assess the goals, virtues, wants, and flaws of the Minervals given to them. As for direction in their work, the members are given a sophisticated set of instructions. Furthermore, as they advance in the Order, the applicants are supposed to work on their gradual purity in life.

Aside from that, members of the Illuminated Minerval grade meet every month to review reports about their allocated groups of Minervals. The Minerval assembly's records are also examined, modified, and finally sent to the Order's top authorities. At this gathering, members also debate ways for achieving the greatest results in their job and seek advice from one another concerning difficult and humiliating incidents.

## Freemasonry and the Illuminati

Weishaupt joined Freemasonry at the lodge of Theodore of Good Counsel in Munich a year after establishing his Illuminati Order. Weishaupt effectively promoted his beliefs in this lodge and encouraged the lodge to join the Illuminist order.

Weishaupt allied the Illuminati and Freemasonry in 1790, when Baron Adolf Franz Friedrich Knigge, a famous German diplomat, and Freemason, was inducted into the Order. In exchange, Knigge's Masonic affiliation and excellent organizing abilities were adopted by the Order. However, Knigge's impact on the Order had two significant repercussions. He was able to restructure the Order's structure by introducing new higher ranks while retaining the originals, and he was able to incorporate Masonic lodges into the system completely.

Knigge merged the Freemasonry ranks into the Illuminati's second degree, making Freemasonry a part of a larger Illuminist framework. The goal was to provide members of the Masonic family from diverse sectors a chance to ascend to higher-order levels. Although Knigge did not modify the Novice of the Order grade, he did include a written statement sent to recruits.

Knigge designed a new method that was acceptable to Freemasons and other powerful persons. As a result, the Order gained significant traction and grew into a formidable movement.

On the other hand, Weishaupt was not able to enjoy the success of his Order for long. The Bavarian government issued an order outlawing all forms of organizations, communities, and brotherhoods that operated without the law's permission. This was in response to widespread concerns that the Illuminati were plotting against political institutions and religious groups across Europe.

Furthermore, there was an internal tension between Weishaupt and the

The Order's higher superiors caused discord and conflicts. Some members opted to go against the Illuminati and testified against the Order before the authorities.

The Bavarian Illuminati were claimed to be disbanded in 1788, twelve years after its formation, due to the government's forceful laws. The Order's members were also charged criminally by the Bavarian authorities. On the other hand, though many felt that the Illuminati had been defeated during this period, it should not be forgotten that the Order had an opportunity to spread beyond the confines of Bavaria. It should be mentioned that the Order was successful in reaching Masonic lodges across Europe. As a result, the Illuminati were never disbanded or annihilated. It was merely underground. In reality, the Illuminati proved to be very much alive and formidable during the French Revolution, a year after it was assumed to be eradicated.

## The French Revolution and the Illuminati

The French Monarchy was brutally abolished in 1789, signifying the failure of old institutions and the triumph of Jacobinism and Illuminism. Later, the Declaration of Human Rights recognized Masonic and Illuminist ideas, incorporating them into the heart of French governance. As a result, the country's new slogan was Liberté, Égalité, et Fraternité, which translates to Freedom, Equality, and Brotherhood. This slogan was used in French Masonic lodges for centuries.

The official paper of the Declaration of Human Rights was constructed of many esoteric symbols. These symbols were thought to represent Secret Societies. The Everything-Seeing Eye was housed inside a triangular emblem, encircled by the light of the blazing star

Sirius, which is placed above all else. An esoteric symbol of a snake swallowing its tail appears underneath the document's title. This sign is known as an Ouroboros, and it is related to Masonry's key principles of Alchemy, Hermetism, and Gnosticism. A crimson Phrygian cap may be discovered just underneath the Ouroboros. This is thought to symbolize Illuminist uprisings all over the globe. Finally, Masonic pillars guard the whole manuscript.

## Protest Against the Illuminati

While many believed the Bavarian Illuminati had been eradicated, the Order's ideas spread across Europe. The Illuminati evidently survived the flourishing Freemasons and Rosicrucians. Europe was undergoing severe unrest at the moment, as a new class of individuals controlled power mechanics. As a result, numerous critics emerged and exposed those responsible for the changes taking place in Europe.

Leopold Hoffman, a Freemason who felt that the Illuminati had corrupted his Brotherhood, was one of the first to speak out against the Illuminati. Hoffmann produced a series of essays in his publication, Wiener Zeitschrift, with various assertions. In one of his writings, Hoffman argued that the French Revolution was the consequence of the Illuminati's long-planned propaganda. He further said that, although the lesser grades of the Illuminati had been eliminated, the top degrees remained operational. Hoffman went on to say that his fraternity, Freemasonry, was being repressed and converted for the Illuminati's advantage.

Following the publication of Hoffman's writings, a slew of newcomers surfaced. In 1797, John Robinson, a Scottish physician, inventor, mathematician, and Freemason, released Proofs of a Conspiracy Against All the Religions and Governments of Europe Carried on in the Secret Meetings of the Freemasons, Illuminati, and Reading Societies. Robinson was a dedicated Freemason who became disillusioned when he discovered that the Illuminati had penetrated his fraternity.

Augustin Barrel, a French Jesuit priest, released his work, Mémoires pour servir à l'histoire du Jacobisime, the same year. The Bavarian Illuminati was linked to the French Revolution, according to Barrel's book. He also decoded the Liberty and Equality phrase, which dates back to the early Templars. According to Barrel, in the upper degrees of the Illuminati, liberty, and equality were presented as a war against kings and throne and a war against Christ and His altars. The barrel also revealed details on the Illuminati's control of Freemasonry.


## The Illuminati's Spread Across America

Most researchers believe that the Founding Fathers of the United States of America were Secret Societies such as Freemasonry, Rosicrucianism, and others. Several of the Founding Fathers journeyed to Europe; they gained insight and vast information about the Illuminati's ideas.

Benjamin Franklin and George Washington were two of the most notable founding fathers alleged to have Illuminist ties.

Benjamin Franklin traveled to Paris as the United States' envoy to France and remained there from 1776 until 1785. The Bavarian Illuminati were particularly active throughout these years. Franklin rose to Grand Master of the Les Neufs Soeurs lodge, which was affiliated with the Grand Orient of France. Franklin's Masonic group was claimed to be the Bavarian Illuminati's headquarters in France. It was also thought to have played a significant role in organizing French support for the American and French revolutions.

George Washington was informed of the Illuminati's goal to bring down all political institutions and religious groups in 1799. German minister G.W. Snyder responded from Washington, stating that he was well aware of the Illuminati's teachings and sinister intentions. However, in his response, Washington also said that he felt no lodges in the United States of America were tainted with the Illuminati's ambitions and ideals. Washington's response made it clear that he was aware of the Illuminati's existence and its values. While Washington thought that the Masonic institutions in the United States remained intact or uncontaminated by the Illuminati's theories, he admitted that certain people might have approved and joined the Illuminati's spread in America.

## Today's Illuminati

In our day and age, the word Illuminati is often used to describe a tiny number of people.

Prominent persons committed to the formation of a One World Government with a common religion and currency. However, it is unclear if this organization is related to the original Bavarian Illuminati or whether its aims and ideals are similar to those of the Weishaupt's Order. On the other hand, many individuals feel that whether or not the name Illuminati refers to the occult elite, the crucial thing to detect is the Illuminati's continuity.

If the Illuminati Order still exists today, the issue now is what shape it will take. Most academics think that several current Secret Societies claim to be heirs of Illuminism, one of which is the Ordo Templi Orientis (OTO). On the other hand, some academics think that there are secret orders that make up the Illuminati and the 33 visible degrees of Freemasonry. Because the Illuminati and Freemasonry are both secret groups, it may be difficult to gain detailed and precise information on both.

As a result, the contemporary Illuminati's political goals are considerably clearer today. According to the researchers, a small group is entrusted with making major choices and policies. There are now worldwide groups and committees that influence elected politicians. Their principal goal is to construct global economic and social policies in which a non-elected shadow government serves as the center of world authority. This government will be made up of elites. This is also getting popular these days.

According to studies on the contemporary Illuminati, the following elite councils and organizations include Chatham House, the World Economic Forum, the Trilateral Commission, the Brookings Institution, and the Bilderberg Group. On the other hand, the Bohemian Club is renowned for holding casual meetings and parties with elites and bizarre rites and rites. The Club's symbol is an owl. As previously stated, the Bavarian Illuminati also employ an Owl, which is the Minerval seal.

Many academics are now discovering that the majority, if not all, of the guests and members of these private clubs are members of the world's elite. The events bring together the most prominent and prominent CEOs, academics, and politicians. The majority of them are scions of great families that control key components of contemporary economies such as the media, financial systems, and oil sector.

According to Fritz Springmeier's book, Bloodlines of the Illuminati, the current Illuminati is made up of the scions of thirteen powerful houses. These families' forebears were known to have had affiliations or affiliations with the original Bavarian Illuminati. The Kennedys, the Rockefellers, the Van Duyns, the Astors, the DuPonts, the Bundys, the Onassis, the Li, the Collins, the Reynolds, the Freemans, the Russells, and the Rothschilds are among the 13 lineages referenced in the book.

Given their political and monetary riches, there is little doubt that some, if not all, of these families wield significant influence globally. It is pretty likely that these families are at the heart of today's Illuminati.

# CHAPTER 4
# THE ILLUMINATI AND MODERN CONSPIRACY THEORIES

Though history records that the Illuminati was disbanded by 1875, some current conspiracy theorists claim that this is inaccurate. Indeed, many of them believe that the Illuminati was never really dissolved. The gang simply moved underground, where they continued to recruit members and promote its views. Doesn't it seem to be innocuous enough? No, not exactly.

The darkest version of this narrative starts with Weishaupt's relocation to Germany. According to history, he spent the remainder of his life as a university lecturer, and when he died, what remained of the order perished with him. Of course, conspiracy theorists will disagree since they believe Weishaupt never stopped communicating with organization members. Throughout that period, he was just putting up a front while promoting enlightenment and advancing the ideology of a one-world government.

**Resurrection:**

According to this thesis, the freethinking order, the same individuals who desired freedom from abuse of power, have subsequently shifted their motivations and are now aiming for global dominance. It sounds a bit far-fetched, doesn't it? These conspiracy theorists argue that if the typical person took more time to study and truly look at what's going on around them, they'd discover that the proof is right there in front of them.

The Illuminati is now more often seen as a hidden conspiracy made up of some of the world's most powerful and wealthy individuals. Out of the darkness,

They allegedly control a large number of individuals in positions of authority and worldwide economic leaders. They penetrate global businesses and countries, rising to the highest levels and obtaining political power and influence. All of this is being done to prepare for the New World Order.

**Impact on Society and History:**

Many hypotheses have been advanced since the inception and alleged disintegration of the Bavarian Illuminati group, blaming the group for several critical events that resulted in major changes. For example, many people think that the Illuminati were responsible for the French Revolution. It was their educated propaganda that lit the fuse and fanned the flames of the revolution. However, this is not the end of the story.

Aside from the French Revolution, the Illuminati is supposed to have engineered a slew of other historical events. Among them are:

- The American War of Independence

- The Assassination of President John F. Kennedy

- Waterloo is an abbreviation for Waterloo, Ontario.

- First World War

- Second World War

- The Ascension of Communism

Every occurrence is alleged to have been orchestrated to weaken global powers and accelerate their dominance. For example, some conspiracy theorists believe that World War I was staged to eliminate Czarism in Russia and ultimately establish the nation as a bastion for Communism. Every move is calculated, and since the rest of the world is uninformed, they may proceed with relative ease.

The same can be said of World War II, which pitted Fascists against so-called political Zionists to strengthen Communism to the point where it surpassed the combined might of Christendom. What about in the future? The Illuminati master plan allegedly includes a World War III, which would pit Muslim or Islamic-ruled states against Western ones. If this succeeds, the conflict would have a devastating effect on the world economy, bringing it to its knees. At this point, the world's various countries would have no option but to surrender to the One World Government system and be ruled by the Illuminati.

Isn't it a terrifying thought? Even worse, many conspiracy theorists think that the Illuminati's influence is all around them and that the New World Order plan is already in motion. Indeed, some argue that we are now seeing the early phases of it, and what will happen if nothing is done to stop it? This New World Order may arrive much sooner than we believe. By the time we may recognize it, it'll be too late.

# CHAPTER 5
# THE ILLUMINATI'S PURPOSE AND OBJECTIVES

The goal of the Illuminati that will be explored in this chapter is based on persons claiming to be members of the Illuminati who break their silence on occasion. They choose certain people to express their thoughts and to challenge those who criticize them. These members, however, say that they are constantly in hiding, as they have always been to protect themselves from those who want to harm them.

On the other hand, the ambitions of the Illuminati that will be discussed in this chapter are based on Dr. John Coleman's book Conspirators' Hierarchy: The Committee of 300, which was published after he traveled to numerous nations to unveil the complete hidden upper-level parallel government. He says that this parallel government governs both the United States of America and the United Kingdom of Great Britain.

**The Purpose of the Illuminati**

According to some putative Illuminati members, the Order's principal goal is to secure human existence in the present. They fear that even the human species will go extinct; thus, people seek to prevent extinction. These putative members contend that, though nations have boundaries, all people are members of the same biological family, making them collective. Furthermore, they argue that every person is critical to the survival of the human race, just as great kings and queens were to their domains.

Humans, according to these supposed Illuminati members, are

Emotion, disharmony, and instinct are all naturally influencing factors. As a result, a human tends to turn on another person for reasons that may not matter in many years. As a result, the Illuminati's mission is to preserve the interests of the human race as a whole. It offers various programs and departments to ensure all ages and from all walks of life. The Illuminati claim to have secured humankind's present domination over other species and predators on Earth.

## Goals of the Illuminati

The Illuminati has created methods and methods to construct a New World Order based on their ideals and values, according to Dr. John Coleman's book Conspirators' Hierarchy: The Committee of 300. Coleman also alleges that the Illuminati formed squads of stooges to carry out their schemes. Coleman stated twenty-one Illuminati aims based on his study and the possibilities he was given to acquiring unique Illuminati papers.

First, the Illuminati seeks to establish a World Government comprised of just one religion and a single currency controlled by the Order.

Second, the Illuminati seeks to obliterate each nation's identity and pride entirely. This is because people will only accept and adopt a super-national global government if these elements are destroyed.

Third, the Illuminati seeks to eradicate all faiths, particularly Christian ones. As a result, the Order will establish just one world religion.

Fourth, the Illuminati seeks to develop thought-control technologies to generate human robots that can respond to external impulses and directions.

Fifth, the Illuminati plans to halt all industrialization systems save the computer and service industries. The idea is to establish a postindustrial society with zero growth, while other sectors will concentrate on third-world nations.

Sixth, the Illuminati plans to encourage and ultimately legalize the use of illegal narcotics and generate art from pornography that will be first approved and then entirely normalized.

Seventh, the Illuminati aims to devastate major cities in the manner of the Cambodian bloodbaths purportedly caused by Pol Pot, a socialist revolutionary.

Eighth, except those fitting the Order's aims and aims, the Illuminati seeks to prohibit future scientific breakthroughs.

Ninth, the Illuminati aims to kill three billion humans prematurely by 2050. This will be accomplished either by famine and disease in developing nations or by regional conflict in rich nations. The Committee of 300 directed the United States Secretary of State during Carter's dictatorship, Cyrus Vance, to submit a study concerning population reduction, precisely how it may be accomplished. President Carter and then-Secretary of State Edwin Muskie recognized and endorsed Vance's document, the Global 2000 Report. According to the Global 2000 Report, one of the requirements is that 100 million people should reduce the US population by 2050.

Tenth, the Illuminati seeks to lower people's morale and discourage the working class via widespread unemployment. As a result, the jobless will be encouraged to use drugs and get addicted to alcohol. Furthermore, the kids will be encouraged to rebel against the status quo, resulting in weaker or split families resulting from drug use and free music.

Eleventh, the Illuminati plans to make people struggle with crisis after a catastrophe to prevent them from determining their destiny. As a result of being overwhelmed by various unpleasant circumstances, the people will learn to rely on the One Government. The Federal Emergency Management Agency (FEMA) already exists as a crisis management entity.

Twelfth, the Illuminati plans to introduce new cults to supplement the current ones.

Thirteenth, the Illuminati plans to foster Protestantism or Christian fundamentalism, ultimately assisting the Zionist Israeli state's interests.

Fourteenth, the Illuminati plans to encourage religious groups like the Sikhs and the Muslim Brotherhood and conduct thought-control experiments. These experiments will be akin to the mass murder/suicide of over 900 persons under the supervision of American cult leader James Warren Jim Jones. Jones instructed his followers to swallow a combination of grape-flavored Flavor Aid and cyanide. He also directed that the same mix be injected into youngsters of a specific age.

Fifteenth, the Illuminati seeks to promote religious freedom by establishing a society in which all other current faiths, particularly Christianity, are questioned and undermined. The Theology of Liberation is regarded to be the Order's starting point.

Sixteenth, the Illuminati plans to agitate the global economy, resulting in utter political chaos.

The Illuminati seek to govern the overall internal and foreign policy of the United States of America on the seventeenth.

The Illuminati want to provide the most support to supranational organizations such as the United Nations Organization (UNO), the Bank for International Settlements (BIS), the International Monetary Fund (IMF), and the International Court of Justice (ICJ), among others. Furthermore, the Illuminati want to deliberately dismantle or put local and national institutions under the supervision of the

United Nations.

On the nineteenth, the Illuminati seek to destabilize and overthrow all governments to split and destroy every nation's sovereignty inside.

Twentieth, the Illuminati intends to foment worldwide terrorism and negotiate with terrorists while carrying out their terrorist acts.

Twenty-first, the Illuminati seeks to control over and finally destroy the educational system of the United States of America.

According to Coleman, the Illuminati's agents functioned and continue to work under the pretext of fighting Zionism and the government.

# CHAPTER 6

# THE SUPPOSED INFLUENCE OF THE ILLUMINATION POPULAR CULTURE

When we think about popular culture, the first things that spring to mind are books, movies, and music - apparently harmless forms of entertainment that we enjoy daily. Would you still be able to look at them the same way after learning that they may be linked to the Illuminati? In this sense, we refer to the alleged hidden cabal hell-bent on global dominance, the group of individuals that conspiracy theorists claim controls things from behind the scenes.

Let's start with movies that are considered to be Illuminati propaganda.

Many conspiracy theorists claim that the order's impact on Hollywood began with Stanley Kubrick's film, Eyes Wide Shut. It was one of the first to advertise and exploit the concept of secret societies. The director's death only months before the film's premiere would add to the debate surrounding the film's Illuminati connections. It has been speculated that Kubrick's dedication to getting the film out there and, in some manner, telling the world about existing secret organizations was what led to his unexplained and untimely death.

The film's depiction of the secret cabal became inextricably linked with the Illuminati itself, with robes, masks, strange rituals, and private gatherings that needed passwords. These items created the public picture of what it's like to be a member of the genuine Illuminati.

Dan Brown's The Da Vinci Code is another film that explores the concept of a hidden conspiracy.

Demons and Angels The novel was adapted into a hit film in 2009, exposing the concept to a far larger audience than Eyes Wide Shut was able to reach. In this thriller, the protagonist races against the clock to prevent the Illuminati, a hidden religious group, from destroying Vatican City. Both sides are shown as having secrets of their own in the film, and the protagonist must learn about some of these secrets to triumph. Finally, the Vatican agrees to take him inside the Vatican's cellars, where the secret archives are housed; everything is safeguarded by bulletproof glass.

What is the truth? The archive does exist. However, it is hidden behind a wing. It is positioned behind St. Peter's Basilica and is said to be a fortification by some. This structure is guarded by a phalanx of Swiss Guards as well as Gendarmerie personnel from the state. Within its walls are 52 kilometers of shelves and old wooden cases, all of which house the church's unique collections of various parchment letters delivered to the Holy See by potentates, rulers, and heretics. It also contains communications between the Vatican and some of history's most famous personalities, including Charlemagne, Erasmus, Mozart, Michelangelo, Voltaire, Queen Elizabeth I, and Adolf Hitler.

So the thought of secrets being kept concealed behind those walls isn't too far-fetched, and it adds to the viewer's belief in the notion. In truth, many individuals have believed the contents of this book to be true, or at the very least to be hints as to what is being kept from them.

Take a closer look at these two flicks now. The hidden order is portrayed as the antagonist of the story in Eyes Wide Shut. On the other hand, Angels and Demons depict them as a group that strives to educate and destroy the hand (the Vatican) that has been concealing all the secrets from the people. Isn't that a remarkable shift? According to conspiracy theorists, it's all part of the propaganda. Instead of frightening people with their secrecy and exclusivity, they're opening themselves up to the general public while maintaining complete control over what is disclosed.

If they need to know who we are, we will be the ones to tell them what they can and cannot know.

They can provide a skewed view of what the organization is about via popular cultural outlets like books, movies, and films—a more romantic, less evil look at their motives and methods to attain their aims. Of course, the strategy is effective. Many individuals are intrigued by the concept, and some have even volunteered to participate. In other ways, the order has become mythological, emanating a feeling of adventure and sincerity that conspiracy theorists claim is all a ruse.

**Shortlist of films on the Illuminati and similar ideals:**

The term "equilibrium" refers to the state of being in a state. In this film, a dictatorship uses pharmaceuticals to numb people's emotions to control the populace.

- V for Vendetta is a film about vengeance. In an all-powerful, dystopian future, the subject of the government's many experiments plans his vengeance against the system that produced him and killed so many others.

- X-Files: Fight For The Future Two FBI agents uncover a worldwide conspiracy to influence and control everyone on the planet's lives.

- 'Star Wars.' An interplanetary conflict was launched by an ambitious politician seeking to consolidate power and establish a global government.

- Nineteen Eighty-Four is a year in the year of the (1984). This film depicts a totalitarian society ruled by a Big-Brother character and its aristocratic Inner Party. To retain its grip on the populace, the establishment employs mind control as well as constant conflicts.

- The Matrix is a science fiction film that was released in 1999. Perhaps the most well-known of the bunch, this film depicts a universe beyond what we know and indicates that everything around us is an illusion.

- The Devil's Advocate A small-town attorney is handed the opportunity of a lifetime, only to learn that the cost is more than he bargained for. Al Pacino plays Satan in this film.

- Tomb Raider is a video game. The film's adversaries are revealed to be members of the Illuminati organization vying to possess an extremely powerful relic. One can only speculate as to what they intend to do with this item.

**The Illuminati's Influence on Music:**

The prevalence of Illuminati-related myths and even its emblems are significantly more visible in the music industry. Numerous artists have begun to experiment with the concept. Conspiracy theorists think that though not everyone in the scene is genuinely linked with the organization, a large percentage of them are. However, contrary to popular belief, they claim that pop singers and artists are only puppets for the Illuminati and are not group members.

Conspiracy theorists claim that, like governments and multinational corporations, the Illuminati has penetrated the top levels of the entertainment business. These are the individuals who make the decisions and have the power to grant or remove any artist's popularity. Consider it as handing your soul over to the devil in return for industry success. All you need to do is follow the orders and promote their misinformation to an even larger audience.

Many prominent singers are claimed to have struck this pact, with Jay-Z and Beyonce being the most well-known. They often incorporate Illuminati symbols during concerts, with Jay-Z adopting the pyramid as a signature hand gesture for his label. Many music videos and song lyrics include images of the Illuminati and the New World Order. At first glance, it may seem to be innocent poetry, but a deeper examination and a better comprehension of the Illuminati purpose will enable a person to see more clearly.

# CHAPTER 7
# BELIEFS OF THE ILLUMINATI

The Illuminati's teachings are founded on four main concepts. These include the tenets of freedom and belief, God and Satan, money and plenty, and value and commerce.

**The Freedom and Belief Tenet**

The Order of the Illuminati has no other beliefs than the sovereignty of the human race. Scholars believe that the Illuminati Order is an elite enterprise of worldwide, prominent, and powerful people rather than a religion, church, charitable organization, or political organization. The Illuminati is supposed to operate only to preserve the interests of the human race; consequently, it is self-governing and unaffiliated with any human division, such as political or religious differences. Given that its mission is to defend the interests of the human species, it functions only for that goal. It does not impose moral, religious, or personal worship requirements on anybody.

The Illuminati believes that all people committed to its purpose, aims, and values are free to pursue their lives as long as they are always in the human race's best interests. Members of the Illuminati are now referred to as Illuminatism adherents, who put aside geographical, generational, and theological boundaries to function as a unified entity with several distinctive elements.

**God's and Satan's tenets**

Faith, according to the Illuminati, is an impression of something that cannot be demonstrated. People observe instructions according to the Order of the Illuminati.

A certain religious scripture from an unverifiable source or an author has never seen or interacted with. Furthermore, many individuals believe in a spiritual being because they were told of miracles by someone who was not even alive when the events occurred.

The Illuminati, on the other hand, says that condemning faith is a stupid act since faith is not limited to religion. The Illuminati's theological basis is founded on the challenging dilemma of faith and skepticism. The Illuminati Order does not speculate on whether or not a deity exists; nevertheless, the Order of the Illuminati's religion is focused on improving the human race on Earth. The Illuminati's choices are based on a study of facts and proof, which are variables that an all-knowing figure may adjust to influence human actions and the future.

The Illuminati refutes the deceptive public idea that the Order is associated with either God or Satan and that many people's misdeeds are under their direction. Furthermore, the Illuminati Order neither recognizes nor rejects any deity and does not regard one as superior to the other. It reiterates that the Order exists to improve the human species.

The Illuminati also denies involvement in horrific crimes such as violent rituals and human sacrifices. The Order professes to be completely committed to preserving humanity, even though its members are free to follow whatever deity they want, given that the Order forbids human sacrifices or any act that violates the maintenance of the human species.

Whether or not a deity is required for its members, the Illuminati merely claims that doing what is best for humanity is what is most important. If there is a greater power, the act of kindness will be rewarded.

## Money and Abundance Tenet

The Illuminati Order believes that a person's worldly influence may be measured in terms of money. According to this exclusive group of influencers, many individuals who have never experienced riches frequently disseminate negative insinuations about money, implying that it is frequently the foundation of all evil. The Illuminati, on the other hand, disagree with this notion, claiming that money may genuinely solve the most agonizing events in one's life. Mothers, for example, utilize the money to meet their children's material necessities. Artists are compensated financially for their trials and years of expertise in their trade. As a result, the Illuminati think that money is not inherently bad.

On the other hand, the Order says that the way money is used good or evil. Since it lacks a voice, soul, or sentiments, money cannot prescribe how it should be utilized. As a result, money may be either beneficial or bad, depending on how it is used. This suggests that just as money may be used to injure someone, it can also be used to cure them. In a more specific example, beggars see money as a food source and life, while tyrants see money as a tool for weapons and even death.

The Illuminati Order believes that everyone should strive for plenty since the Earth is filled with resources for everyone to enjoy. The Order compares a prosperous life to a drink of water. If you like, life is rich.

The glass is filled to the brim with water, which pours over the sides. As a result, when a person enjoys an abundant life, he or she has the flexibility to assist others since he or she no longer needs to assist himself or herself.

Regarding the relationship between money and plenty, the Illuminati thinks that money may be measured by those who carry it. For example, a hundred dollars is a lot for a beggar; a hundred dollars is a lot for a millionaire; hundreds of thousands enable a billionaire to save lives by providing necessities such as food, shelter, and medication. However, if a person is destitute or has a limited life, he or she cannot rescue anybody, even himself or herself.

## Value and Trade Principle

The Order of the Illuminati regards things that are free as worthless. However, the majority of charges do not need payment in the form of money. A strong intellect, for example, costs a person's hours spent learning and reading. A healthy physique requires a person's work and time spent preparing to eat and exercising. The Illuminati, on the other hand, thinks that money offers a numerical value to nearly everything on Earth, making money a marketable commodity of both labor and knowledge.

According to the Illuminati Order, the main function of money is to provide a mathematical value to work and understanding of the trade. A legal student, for example, pays money to a school to get the information needed for his future vocation. The lawyer's information received from professors is remunerated financially. Money may be used to pay for other people's efforts and expertise in the future, even if they do not need the services of a lawyer.

As a result, the Illuminati's concept about value and trade is that things of value are never free; otherwise, they are worthless.

# CHAPTER 8
# SYMBOLISM, RITUALS, AND OCCULTISM IN THE ILLUMINATI

The Illuminati and its rituals are connected with a wide range of symbols. Many of these symbols may be observed regularly and go undetected unless you open your attention to their various potential meanings.

**Here is a handful of the most well-known:**

- On top of a pyramid, there is an all-seeing eye. This combo is one of the Illuminati's most prominent emblems. The eye represents the Illuminati rule, while the pyramid represents the power structure, with a small number at the top and a large number at the bottom.

- The pentagram has been reversed. Many see it as a sign of evil since it depicts the deity of the underworld attacking heaven with his horns pointing skyward.

- The all-seeing eye This signifies the Illuminati's capacity to see and control everything. It is also believed that it demonstrates their ability to be everywhere, infiltrating many various areas to sow the seeds of their master plan.

- Owls are a kind of bird. For many different civilizations, an owl represents wisdom. However, in Illuminati symbology, it signifies the order's enlightened state of mind. They consider themselves to be the smartest and hence must dominate the world. The Minerva emblem has also been utilized by the elite of the Bohemian Grove as well as the Minervals of the Bavarian Illuminati.

- Obelisks are a kind of monument. Obelisks are used to denote the many centers of power of the Illuminati. It has been used to demonstrate military supremacy in Washington, D.C. It is thought that the ones in New York and London signify their financial dominance.

## What is the significance of these symbols?

Just look at how many celebrities have adopted the one-eyed emblem and turned it into a fad that the public has embraced. The all-seeing eye is represented by the picture of one eye being visible and the other being covered. Celebrities such as Lady Gaga, Kim Kardashian, and Rihanna have utilized this motif multiple times, making it a prominent position that many others attempt to imitate.

Another common hand gesture is the Okay sign, which also represents the number six. Without the context of the Illuminati, this hand motion is often used to express that everything is alright or that I am OK. However, for members of the Illuminati, it represents the Triple six or the number of the beast. In other words, it is a promise of devotion to Satan as well.

Aside from this, several forms of secret handshakes that members of the order utilize to welcome one another. However, more often than not, these handshakes are just for higher-ranking members to know and not for everyone to know.

## The Rituals of the Illuminati:

One may imagine an organization that seems so contemporary and focused would have no purpose for old rites. According to conspiracy theorists, this is most definitely not the case with the Illuminati. In reality, their rites are identical to those used millennia ago, beginning with animal sacrifices. Why is this the case? The Illuminati believe in the spiritual world, and by connecting with it via these rituals, they hope to gain control of the energies that drive it all. More power keeps these folks in business for a longer period.

According to conspiracy theorists, the Illuminati has six major areas of study. Sciences and spirituality are two of the most significant, but they are also the most distinct. It has also been said that regardless of the department a member comes from, they are obligated to participate in spiritual rites on high days. This is a key feature of their membership in the order.

The Celtic spiritual branch believes that power is transferred during the transition between life and death. This is the focal point of one rite in which adults and children are bound and bled on top of them. They believe that by doing so, the individual will get strength from the animal's departed soul.

It should be noted that all of this material has been disseminated by conspiracy theorists, and it, like many other beliefs linked with the Illuminati, has never been confirmed conclusively.

# CHAPTER 9
# SYMBOLS OF THE ILLUMINATI

The Illuminati Order employs symbols, which most people associate with artwork, visual media, and architecture. The Illuminati, on the other hand, claims that its emblems serve as lofty teachings for those who choose to follow the Light. This chapter will go through each sign in-depth to help you grasp what they symbolize.

## Pyramid of Giza

The Illuminati uses the Pyramid as a symbol to show that everyone is a member of the most complicated process. Each level of the Pyramid is critical; without it, there would be no structure at all. The Pyramid serves as a reminder to everyone that the path of life starts at the bottom. Only a handful, however, climb above or proceed to the next level. As a person progresses up the Pyramid, he or she becomes more conscious of his or her role on Earth.

## The Observer

The Illuminati uses the Eye as a symbol to represent someone who sees and knows everything. It is at the heart of the Light. According to the Illuminati Order, the Light is set on truth, and those who follow it become the core of our planet's Universal Design. The Illuminati describe the Eye as a shepherd who sees and understands his whole flock.

## The Sunlight

The Illuminati uses the Light as a symbol to represent ever-present guidance in a world fraught with adversity, conflict, and misunderstanding. Everyone is looking for the

The Light's brilliance reflects it into the world's dark places. Similarly, individuals who follow it to better humanity will be rewarded by an invisible and unidentified greater authority.

## The Infinite/Circle

The Illuminati uses the Eternal or Circle as a symbol to indicate its commitment to the world, which has withstood millennia and the most traditional political entities. According to them, although the Illuminati's operations are rarely recognized or acknowledged, they continue to affect key movements on Earth. The Order claims to be leading and preserving the human species from extinction. The Eternal represents the Illuminati's ability to stand forever.

# CHAPTER 10
# THE ILLUMINATI'S POLITICAL AGENDA

The British Empire is a Freemasons' Empire, much as the Portuguese Empire was an Order of Christ Empire. Above this Empire are the so-called Illuminati, who are just as educated as those under them. In other words, we're talking about individuals who are very powerful, egotistical, mentally ill, and arrogant, and who would make their forefathers embarrassed of their deeds and abuse of historical symbols. They should be called Shadows of the Illuminati instead because nothing is enlightening about them. This term has also been misused so that the masses are led to believe that their power is legitimate and do not resist when the time comes for them to rule over the world in Communist style.

While people are still persuaded to think that politicians and monarchs control them, an unseen government sits enthroned behind the transparent government, owing no loyalty and accepting no accountability to the people (President Theodore Roosevelt). The world is run by people who are extremely different from those who are not behind the scenes" (British Prime Minister Benjamin Disraeli). Today, the Illuminati organization, often known as the shadow government, entirely controls the key forces of international security and espionage, such as the CIA, FBI, Europol, and MI5. It functions in such a subtle manner that we scarcely realize how the control grows. If a leader is impervious to corruption, he will be assaulted first with rumors, slain strangely, or imprisoned on bogus charges. The people' emotional disassociation and apathy in their leaders and most renowned prophets

It remains one of the most used instruments for mass control.

The notion is arrogant, as they feel that man has survived for a long period based on adaptability and that what is required today in anticipation. (Meeting of the Bilderbergs, 1969)

This was originally attributed to a religious leader in China, a Zen Buddhism monk. It began with compulsion about installing hidden cameras within the temple and modifying his worldview with the collaboration of political authorities to conform it to a shared government ideal. But he refused, arguing that it was against his ideals, and publicly notified his supporters about the effort to corrupt him. So, one day, his phone vanished, and manipulated photographs and texts were sent from it to his followers and his internet homepage, in which he allegedly described himself as having orgies in his meditation classes. In several photos, he was even seen with infants who were said to be his own.

Because they were afraid of the implications, the other Buddhists in the group remained silent about the reality, and this monk was compelled to renounce his life in the temple, his leadership, and his status as a monk. In his final actual post, he claimed that he was abandoned by his followers in a pit of falsehoods in otom his name and that this was the why

Another thing that the Chinese Communist Government does is create Smartphone applications in the form of games that citizens believe have the purpose of catching criminals in exchange for monetary rewards, but promote their cooperation in catching political dissidents by harassing people in public photographing anyone they see. To get a sense of how intrusive and abusive such a society is, try to sit on a public vehicle and have everyone take photographs of you the whole time while examining your background. In reality, these programs are advertised on train and metro TV displays to entice passengers to download them.

This Chinese government approach is supported by the assumption that we are already living in a post-information age. It is no longer the quantity of information one has or has access to that matters but one's capacity to sort and use it. In modern culture, the most important commodity is attention - the capacity to demand it and the willingness to offer it (Arno A. Penzias at the Bilderberg Meeting, 1995). On the other hand, the power elite thinks that every political, military, or economic action taken by a nation must have popular approval. It is our leaders' job to clearly and rationally define the changing environment we now confront, as well as the necessity to bring our various security systems up to date (Manfred Worner at the Bilderberg Meeting, 1993).

As we can see, nobody will be secure anywhere in such a society since everyone would be enemies to themselves, and fighting the system would be almost impossible. As in contemporary China, the citizenry would be both the captives and the jail guards.

Another advantage of smartphones is that they allow people to be tracked anywhere in the world, collecting personal information about them, such as websites they visit and messages they send and read, but also allowing hackers to hack into their private lives and do absolutely anything with it, including criminalizing them for things they haven't done. The issue with the future now is that it is not what it used to be (Paul Valery), which implies that such a future is in the hands of a chosen and extremely strong few. Today, the road to absolute tyranny may be paved using only legal methods (Senator William Jenner).

# CHAPTER 11

# THE ILLUMINATI'S STRATEGY

The Illuminati of contemporary times are members of the rich elite from all over the globe. Their activities are based on various other historic organizations associated with enlightenment and gnostic traditions, such as the Knights Templar, the Rosicrucians, the Satanists, and the Druids. They've arranged their ideas and practices to support their best interests rather than to enhance spirituality or compassion as human beings. The Illuminati, as a religious institution, is founded on egoistical ideals and hence supports the evil side of the human soul, also known as the tree of death in Kabbalah. In doing so, he challenges the old Illuminati, meaning modern-day Rosicrucians, Freemasons, Scientologists, Buddhists, Hindus, and so on. That is why they seek to eradicate all faiths and unify them under their light and regulations. Politically and financially, the Illuminati think that global governments and political sovereignty are doomed. They seek to replace such governments via their sub-societies, such as the Bilderberg group.

The Bilderberg Group believes that cooperation among central bankers is preferable to benign neglect; that policymakers must exercise discipline - both in strengthening economic fundamentals and in maintaining a consistent public stance when intervening in currency markets; that regulation or controls will not work; and that a credible alternative to the dollar as a reserve currency is desirable (Hilmar Kopper at the Bilderberg Meeting, 1995). During their discussions, "There are no resolutions to be debated or voted on. The goal of the discussion is to provide a full overview of the issues on the Agenda, from which each participant is allowed to develop his or her judgments. However, it is anticipated that people who attend the meetings would be better prepared to utilize their power to enhance global relations. As a result, the press and the general public are barred from attending, and no background documents or speeches are made available " (Notice to Participants in the

Bilderberg Meeting of 1974).

Despite the secrecy, it is now apparent that the first step of the strategy is to expand mass debt by manipulating equities and interest rates. And since most people will be unable to pay their loans at some time, national banks will go bankrupt, which is why we see so many unexpectedly shut doors throughout the globe, particularly in Europe's poorest countries, such as Portugal and Spain. Every time this happened, individuals lost their whole life's savings, which vanished from their accounts and ended up in the hands of the Power Elite, the debt collectors.

When people begin rioting in the streets and mass demonstrations against their governments, a state of emergency will be declared, legitimizing military involvement and the implementation of martial rule. Nato and other international forces will be called in to intervene until a solution that guarantees peace among all nations is presented. This solution will be designed by the bankers and leaders of this Illuminati order before orchestrating world chaos, following one of their favorite quotes and Illuminati premise, ordo ab Chao, which means order out of chaos.

While some may believe that resistance is conceivable, it is important noting that many Illuminati members are currently or have been military commanders and politicians who are highly trained in warfare and understand how to utilize surprise to their advantage. Following the military takeover, the general populace will be faced with just two alternatives. Opposing the new order may result in imprisonment, torture, and death, as shown in the stories of the Soviet Union, Nazi Germany, and Mao Zedong's revolution. History will repeat itself because the general population remains in the dark, ignorant of the facts, ignorant of how the world truly works, and unwilling to understand how to protect itself while being distracted by distractions that oppose it within itself, such as racism, discrimination, and other distinguishing conflicts, which prevent everyone from seeing what is happening beyond this duality, from t

In their hubris, the Illuminati leaders think that the great majority of the populace are nothing more than mindless sheep who, like in Communist China today, will be readily led if given strong leadership and financial assistance, but also if harshly punished for disobeying.

Hillary Clinton, who is being backed by the banking elite to become the next President of the United States and launch a global war against Russia and other countries, summarized this strategy perfectly when she said: "We simply can't trust people to make decisions." The government must make decisions for the people. It's time for a fresh start. We must shift our focus away from the individual and toward what is beneficial for society.

According to various sources, the Illuminati order's reigning families, particularly the Rothschilds, Rockefellers, Carnegies, Mellons, and Vanderbilts, are the same families who supported Clinton's campaign and will be the ones proposing answers to the chaotic world they are constructing. A new monetary exchange system will be established, based on an international monetary system and a virtual currency. The same individuals will organize and safeguard the world's economic and political leadership. They argue that it is impossible to have independent monetary policies, fixed rates, and capital mobility; one of these, monetary independence, must be sacrificed, which implies one currency (Bilderbert Meeting, 1995).

# CHAPTER 12
# ENLIGHTENMENT THROUGH THE ILLUMINATI

The Illuminati's vision of enlightenment is based on an interpretation of the Kabbalah's last spiritual level, the crown. The crowned man is not afraid of darkness and may even utilize it to promote light. He is not afraid of suffering or death because he recognizes their significance and goal in the larger dynamic of events that life needs to progress. Furthermore, he does not see the law as an oppressive instrument but rather as a method to achieve a correct equilibrium on Earth. That is why he does not love in the human sense but rather in the divine sense. If necessary, he will demolish to develop and construct something greater. If there is no peace to preserve, such people do not send peacekeepers (Peter Carrington at the Bilderberg Meeting, 1995).

A guy with such a mentality and despises humanity with its silly habits, rituals, and wants is sometimes labeled a fool. In contrast, in reality, he commands the energy of the sport and the magician, both powers beyond what humanity's eyes can perceive. The fool has no earthly commitments and is free to think honestly and without the constraints of assumption and illusion. The magician knows the relationship between material and spiritual, and he or she can create anything at command. He has power over the physical universe, which he uses to manipulate people's thoughts, deluded fears, and desires, as well as their five sense-based beliefs about reality.

This is the reason why "without the shift of business from the regional and national to the global level, as well as the systematic development of technology,

supported by a concurrent investigation into man's inner reality and personality harmony, can only lead to a regression through a return to even more restricted positivism than that of Auguste Comte and

Littré " (Dr. Henri Hartung at the Bilderberg Meeting, 1968). And so, ideally, the crowned man is superior to all human beings, not because he is superior to them, but because he has, through his actions and the honesty of his truthful insights, both acquired with the conscience of the laws of cause and effect, and the comprehensive study of metaphysical knowledge, detached from the importance that life on earth has for its reincarnated souls, which persist I

The crowned man has no such attachments and is happy in his delight of freedom while absorbing the full meaning of his spiritual existence, like a bodhisattva who does not require life but lives to assist others in living better lives. That is why we name this state a crowned state since the king is the only one who can serve the kingdom. This kingdom belongs to God, the parent of many kingdoms (as Jesus stated when referring to his many dwellings), yet it has enough space for many kings. Indeed, humans were designed to be the rulers of this kingdom, which entails serving nature and life in general and His desire for the kingdom.

Most individuals will never comprehend these truths because they have poor life judgment and only limited their spiritual freedom. The majority of individuals do not relocate. They live and die within a few kilometers of their birthplace (Philip Martin at the Bilderberg Meeting, 1993). Money may be significant in their society. Still, it should never replace the power that an awakened soul has over it since it is merely a physical form of existence, an illusion like many others manufactured by people to trap humanity. And it is for this reason; the crowned man must learn to govern money while also separating from it since his independence is dependent on such a balanced attitude.

We may find it difficult to break out from this worldview. As a result, for many, the duality of life is founded on the unpleasant truth that a person who is unable to purchase the work that he desires suffers inconvenience or a drop in earnings, while a person who is unable to sell his work is effectively informed that he is of no use. The first issue is discomfort or loss, whereas the second is a personal disaster (Sir William Beveridge at the Bilderberg Meeting, 1995). Nonetheless, let us continue to strive for unlimited prosperity while remaining focused on our objective since prosperity will permeate all of our lives while providing us pleasure and freedom. Above all, we must remember that capitalism without bankruptcy is analogous to Christianity without damnation" (Bilderberg Meeting, 1995).

# CHAPTER 13
# THE ILLUMINATI AND FREEMASONRY LINK

When it comes to strong secret societies, another group whose name is nearly associated with the Illuminati, despite allegations that they are wholly separate organizations, comes to mind.

The Freemasons are a fraternal society that predates the original Bavarian Illuminati. Their beginnings may be traced back to the stonemasons' local fraternities, which were founded to regulate a mason's credentials as well as their relationships with both authorities and customers. The similarity with the Illuminati derives from the fact that the two have many parallels and have crossed paths on several occasions.

There may be a link between the Freemasons and the Illuminati, although it might be difficult to prove. It is widely assumed that an Illuminati delegate attended a Freemason conference in 1782. This occurred at Wilhelmsbad, Hesse, Germany, and was sanctioned and protected by the Duke of Brunswick. However, it should be emphasized that Freemasons are a considerably older organization, has been since the 16th century, and sharing the same practice of enlightened principles as the Illuminati. They believe in all men's equality as well as the presence of a Supreme Being. Charity is another something that the Freemasons do regularly. Certain customs may change from one lodge to the next, but the members' commitment is cemented by an oath, a vow to the brotherhood.

Another resemblance between the two orders is that they are magnets for debate, persecution, and criticism. There are conspiracy theorists who believe that the Freemasons and the Illuminati are pursuing global dominance. They control the shots and govern the world from behind the scenes. One of the emblems used by the masons is the all-seeing eye.

A British author called John Robinson reportedly exposed the relationship between the two orders. In 1798, he published a book that revealed all of the ties between various factions and the developing plot against Europe's governments and faiths. His work, along with Abbot Agustin Barruel's, blamed Adam Weishaupt entirely for his membership in the Bavarian Illuminati and the propagation of Enlightenment ideas. Both writers were royalists who claimed that the French Revolution was the work of many organizations, including the Freemasons and the Illuminati. The writers argued that they impacted the minds of the satisfied peasants and changed them from religion to atheism, from decency to dissoluteness, and from zealous allegiance to lethal revolt.

But are these assertions true? No, not exactly. The idea that secret societies impacted and contributed to the spirit of the French Revolution is not completely baseless. Consider that the more rationalist Freemasons, together with the Illuminati, constituted a substantial danger to the European oligarchies of the period, all of which relied on the authority of the Roman Catholic Church for legitimacy. Numerous historians think that many secret organizations made it their mission to disseminate anti-monarchist views and publicly criticize the church. According to these secret organizations, the church was an obstacle to progress, scientific advancement, and true freedom. However, it has not been shown that they were the fundamental cause of the revolution itself.

**The Primary Distinction Between the Orders:**

If we compare the Illuminati to the Freemasons, the most obvious distinction between the two is their overarching purpose as an order.

According to several conspiracy theories, the Illuminati seeks to construct a New World Order that would fundamentally alter how the world operates. The Freemasons, on the other hand, aspire to establish a new kind of society in which honor and chivalry are highly valued. They are not interested in gaining power over the people but rather in bringing about positive change.

# CHAPTER 14
# THE ILLUMINATI CONSPIRACY THEORIES THAT ARE POPULAR

Countless conspiracy theories regarding the Illuminati have emerged throughout the years, ranging from the credible to the truly strange. We'll go through some of the most well-known ones that many people think to be true on this list.

## The 9/11 Atrocity

Considered one of the most heinous terrorist acts on American soil, many conspiracy theorists think the Illuminati carried it out to spark a new global war. This tragedy happened to be the defining moment for the US government when it comes to fighting terrorism.

## The assassination of John F. Kennedy

Even though it has been several years after the assassination of JFK, there is still much controversy and discussion regarding it. Some claim they accept the government's claims, while others argue there are many contradictions in these claims that have never been fully resolved. Some think that JFK was assassinated because he attempted to reveal the Illuminati's influence on the government. He was the pawn that refused to obey instructions, and as such, he had to be removed.

## 'Celebrity Pawns'

Today's top superstars have undeniable power and influence. They can persuade you to purchase something or even believe in a concept. Some conspiracy theorists claim that some of these celebrities are being used as puppets by the Illuminati. They're disseminating misinformation in subtle and not-so-subtle ways. With the next generation enthralled by their every action and attempting to imitate it, this is undoubtedly one of the finest methods to spread the word, and the Illuminati is taking full advantage. Consider how many celebrities display Illuminati symbology in their behaviors, performances, music videos, and even song lyrics.

## Dumbing Down The People

It's no secret that the ordinary person knows more about a celebrity's life than they do about what's going on around them. According to conspiracy theorists, this is also part of the Illuminati's overall plan - a strategy to divert people's attention so that no one notices their moves. The Illuminati is supposed to control the media that spread celebrity news, forcing them to publish even the tiniest news on a certain personality incessantly. In the middle of all the irrelevant information, the average population is always oblivious of what is vital.

## Murders of Celebrities

Most people would consider celebrity deaths to be sad but not out of the usual. Certain deaths, however, are said to be the work of the Illuminati, according to conspiracy theorists. This relates to celebrities who may have found something they shouldn't have and want to disclose it. Some celebrities may have refused to cooperate in the Illuminati's schemes and were finally destroyed because they were no longer useful to the organization. People like Princess Diana and Amy Winehouse may have perished at the hands of the Illuminati, but the murder was carefully hidden.

## Mind Control Software

When it comes to the Illuminati, this is one of the darker conspiracy ideas. It entails using mind control and programming to force individuals to obey their commands without doubt or hesitation. Consider the use of persons who no longer control their ideas and behaviors for different propaganda reasons. According to some conspiracy theorists, celebrities may have experienced this kind of programming, and the alterations are obvious in the way their careers have surged at an alarming rate.

Aside from celebrities, others believe that politicians have also been subjected to this sort of brainwashing and that they are only acting as a front for the Illuminati goal.

# CHAPTER 15
# THE ILLUMINATI TREE'S BRANCHES

If you want to see what would happen to a world controlled by the Illuminati Order, go to Modern Communist China and see how brainwashed people live their lives, controlled by fear and surveillance in every corner of every city and village, how a nation controlled by the power of genocide and unprecedented death sentences, mostly used for political purposes, has given up dreaming. Because it is the perfect framework for the world, according to the Illuminati. David Rockefeller, the creator of the Bilderberg Society, said in an interview: "Whatever the cost of the Chinese Revolution, it has succeeded not just in establishing a more efficient and devoted government, but also in generating high morale and community of purpose." Under Chairman Mao's guidance, China's social experiment was one of the most significant and successful human histories.

However, we can't declare that the Illuminati have complete power over every leader and country since several have rebelled against the system since then. History is seldom as linear as it seems, and religion is no exception. For example, Christianity was divided into two branches. Mary Magdalene fled to France, and Peter, who had stolen Jesus' established authority, felt that he was the one to go on and preserve his legacy. As a result of this, her reputation was permanently ruined, as were Jesus' ideals. Today's Bible is built on gnostic writings that were mistranslated after others were destroyed or rejected for not conforming to the ideas of the Popes who were responsible for its abuse. And, given that none of the Popes is genuine, we cannot conclude that the Christian Bible was ever founded on truth. In one of the lost Gospels, Peter is described as stating the Gospel of Thomas, "Make Mary leave us because females do not deserve life." And in The Pistis Sophia, he writes, "We are not able to tolerate this lady who deprives us of our chance."

What was Peter alluding to when he said "opportunity"? In mainstream Christianity, Mary Magdalene is portrayed as a contrite sinner and redeemed prostitute, but in Gnosticism, she is regarded as the Christian Church's head. Jesus loved her more than the other disciples (The Gospel of Philip) and more than the other women (The Gospel of Mary), and said to her, Mary, thou blessed one, whom I will complete in all the secrets (The Pistis Sophia), for I have given you dominion over all things and Sons of Light (The Sophia of Jesus Christ).

Illuminati is derived from both Jesus' and Mary Magdalene's remarks since people who do not understand the secrets of the light are said to be in the dark and unable to see. Mary Magdalene declares in The Gospel of Mary, "What is concealed from you, I shall announce to you."

Other faiths' stories aren't much different. Buddhists have long contested the legitimacy of the Dalai Lama, and debates between schools such as Gelug and Nyingma continue to this day. Although being one of the most respected Illuminati members today, Aleister Crowley died penniless and without any followers around him. However, one individual who studied his teachings thoroughly would ultimately earn a greater reputation, powerful enough to warrant the same technique used when a church gets as huge as Scientology, the world's fastest-growing church. The creator of Scientology, Ron Hubbard, was persecuted, and his reputation is still under assault over thirty years after his death. During his lifetime, the FDA (an organization controlled by the Illuminati order and conducting mass population reduction using texts like the Codex Alimentarius) stole all of his works, and he died under strange circumstances. Mr. David Miscavige, who took his position and is now heading his Church, got rid of the top Scientologists by utilizing whatever unlawful methods he could, burnt L. Ron Hubbard's will, and lied about it. Then, as President of the Church, he discovered a legal mechanism to eliminate the remainder of the members who were opposed to him, who in most instances created the Freezone Society, a group of L. Ron Hubbard study followers with an autonomous structure.

The OTO (Ordo Templaris Orientis) may have retained the copyrights to Aleister Crowley's original publications. Still, it is not a descendent of the Knights Templar, nor are any other groups claiming it. The Templars, having discovered the gnostic texts and realized the Vatican's falsehoods and true history, chose to defend genuine Christianity and its heritage via Mary Magdalene and the descendants of Christ, and new orders, such as the OTO, claim to be descendants only for this purpose. However, there is a wanted relation between mysticism and reality that is not always genuine and, once again, perverts truth.

The Templars were wealthy and powerful, prone to corruption; they were the financiers of the biggest European conflicts, subjected to rulers' private interests, ultimately bringing them to an end. Many Templars were persecuted and burnt alive, while others formed three major organizations: the Freemasons, the Knights of Malta, and the Order of Christ, amalgamated with Rosicrucian traditions. The Order of Christ engaged in sea-borne expansion via Portugal for two reasons: more wealth and the establishment of a new global order that would eventually overthrow the control of the Vatican, Europe's most powerful institution at the time. This order is mostly what inspires modern-day bankers.

The Freemasons, on the other hand, desired sovereignty of Europe and collaborated with the Vatican in arrangements that led to the Napoleonic Wars and the two World Wars. Because of these events, the remaining Knights of Malta were compelled to merge with the Freemasons and migrate. Their cross, which can now be found in the paintings of most European aristocrats, now has a different significance.

The masonic method was lengthy and bloody. And the internal battle has undermined the Order of Christ more swiftly, mostly via its employment of piracy and the support of rebellions in countries that were formerly members of this new world, thereby creating divisions amongst them to weaken the nations and prepare for a future invasion. This was the fate of the old Portuguese colonies, which were taken over by the British, Dutch, and French, all of whom were influenced by Freemason principles. These three nations remain at the core of the Freemasons' political agenda, explaining why there is so much economic interdependence between them. And yet, we can't blame the Freemasons as much as we can condemn their leaders and their true aims since not all Freemasons understand what their organizations at the top of the hierarchy are all about. Many Freemasons may claim to be free of political propaganda. Still, we also know that many politicians are freemasons, and the lodges of freemasonry profit from an autonomous administration between them. In other words, each lodge is free to promote the values it desires and to choose its members based on independent criteria. A person might be chosen by one lodge and rejected by another, or, from the Freemasons' perspective, merit exclusion due to a lack of morals in his lifestyle but avoiding elimination due to crucial links to other organization members.

# CHAPTER 16

# THE THEORY OF THE ILLUMINATI

## Brief Synopsis

Many individuals nowadays are interested in the Illuminati and share good and bad information about the Order, particularly on the Internet. The majority of the material surfacing now is regarding the Illuminati's influence globally, politics, entertainment, and media.

Even before technological advancements, writers and conspiracy theorists claimed that the Illuminati Order still existed, although in secret, as it had done since its inception. Augustin Barruel, David Icke, William Guy Carr, Mark Dice, and Nesta Helen Webster are among the writers and conspiracy theorists. In addition, Webster's thesis holds that an elite Jewish group manages the Illuminati to propagate capitalism and communism, dividing the globe and finally ruling it.

Many other theories think about secret organizations, notably the Illuminati, and each hypothesis is unique. For example, Christian fundamentalists believe that the One World Government, or, in current parlance, the Illuminati's New World Order, heralds the approach of the antichrist. The John Birch Society, an American political advocacy organization, endorsed this thesis by defining the goal of secret organizations such as the Illuminati.

Some of the most talked-about incidents related to Illuminati conspiracies will be covered in this chapter. In addition, a list of celebrities who are reportedly Illuminati members, as well as those who the Order has reportedly silenced, will be released.

## Famous Illuminati Conspiracies and (Alleged) Illuminati Conspiracies

### 9/11: A Tragedy

The 9/11 or Twin Tower Tragedy was one of the most violent and tragic incidents in the history of the United States of America. Most conspiracy theories attribute the catastrophe to the meticulous plot devised by the Illuminati. The tragedy prompted the United States Government to declare war on worldwide terrorism, and when the government needs funding to battle its opponents, it was exposed to the Illuminati. According to conspiracy theorists, secret groups' methods are to give out forecasts about their intentions. Before the 9/11 catastrophe, the Cartoon Network's Johnny Bravo cartoon series broadcast an episode strikingly similar to the catastrophe.

### Puppeteers in the Media

According to conspiracy theorists, most individuals know more about their favorite celebrity than their neighbors or coworkers. According to these theories, all of this is part of the Illuminati's propaganda, which controls and manipulates the media. Such control aims to disseminate obsessive and ludicrous celebrity news to divert public attention away from more serious issues such as the government, revolutions, global politics, and rebellions. As the general population loses sight of these issues, the Illuminati gains access to people's hearts and minds.

### Mysterious Assassinations and Deaths of Famous People: Conspiracy Theories

Most conspiracy theorists also link the Order of the Illuminati to the strange deaths and killings of notable people not just in the United States but all across the world.

## Lincoln, Abraham

The Illuminati allegedly planned to murder Lincoln to prevent him from aggressing against large enterprises and companies, which the latter saw as a danger to him and the Southern Confederacy. The Illuminati arranged the killing to prevent Lincoln from speaking out against the Order. Lincoln's words were cited: "In times of peace, the money forces prey on the country, and in times of misfortune, they plot against it. The financial powers are more oppressive than a monarchy, arrogant than autocracy, and self-centered than a bureaucracy. They label as public enemy anybody who questions their tactics or sheds light on their misdeeds." As a result, Lincoln was assassinated on April 15, 1865.

## Kennedy, John F.

The 35th President of the United States was reported to have worked with the Illuminati, but, as he began to oppose the Order's aims and tactics, his murder was planned. JFK was shot twice in the head and once in the neck on November 22, 1963.

## Oswald, Lee Harvey

The sharpshooter who murdered JFK was also claimed to be an Illuminati victim. During JFK's assassination, Oswald was said to be under the Illuminati's mind control. Oswald, on the other hand, was apprehended by the police. To

On November 24, 1963, two days after JFK's murder, Oswald was shot as he would be transported to a county prison to prevent him from revealing the mastermind of JFK's killing.

## Martin Luther King, Jr.,

Because of his power, this individual posed a danger to the Illuminati. According to conspiracy theories, MLK started protesting the Vietnam War, which brought huge financial advantages to numerous firms at the time. As a result, the Illuminati devised a scenario for MLK's assassination. On April 4, 1968, he was shot on the balcony of a Memphis hotel.

## John F. Kennedy, Jr.,

Conspiracy theorists can't help but relate JFK Jr.'s death to his father, JFK, and think it was all part of the Illuminati's plan. Rumors proliferated around the United States concerning JFK, Jr.'s knowledge of his father's death. Rumors circulated that George H. W. Bush and the CIA were involved in JFK's killing. JFK, Jr. was claimed to be ready to share the information he had when his jet inexplicably crashed. The jet crashed owing to a pilot mistake, according to reports. JFK, Jr. had wanted to be a pilot since he was a youngster, so he took flying classes and obtained his pilot's license. JFK, Jr. was assassinated with his wife and sister-in-law.

## The Beatles' John Lennon

Because he was a member of a world-famous band, John Lennon was considered a danger by many prominent and powerful individuals. The Immigration and Naturalization Service (INS) did try to deport Lennon. He was also under monitoring by the Federal Bureau of Investigation (FBI). Apart from being a rock celebrity, John Lennon was also a political activist and a peace campaigner. He also recorded anti-war songs. Mark David Chapman, Lennon's killer, is alleged to have been linked with the Illuminati and under their mind control when he assassinated Lennon on December 8, 1980.

## Malcolm X was a revolutionary.

Malcolm X, an American Muslim clergyman and human rights activist, was a major danger to the Illuminati Order. He was dubbed "the most powerful African American who was hostile to the power system." Malcolm X was shot with a sawed-off shotgun and semi-automatic pistols on February 21, 1965, as he prepared to speak to the Organization of Afro-Americans in Manhattan.

## Jim Morrison is a rock musician.

Many conspiracy theorists claim Morrison was a reptilian member of the Illuminati Order. Through his song, he supported hippie counterculture revolt and the generational divide. Furthermore, his death remains uncertain. Morrison allegedly died of a heart attack on July 3, 1971, although his death was not publicized until three days later. Furthermore, numerous individuals claim to have seen Morrison in seedy locations worldwide following his purported death. The majority of conspiracy theorists think that the Illuminati staged Morrison's death.

## Bruce Lee is a martial artist.

Lee is widely regarded as the most influential martial artist of all time, and he is also credited with changing the way Asians were portrayed in American films. Before his death on July 20, 1973, Lee often warned others that a demon was watching him. He died as a result of an adverse reaction to a pain reliever. However, conspiracy theorists think Lee was a sacrifice for the Illuminati.

## Grace Kelly is a well-known actress.

Most conspiracy theorists think that Kelly's marriage to Rainier III, Prince of Monaco, was orchestrated by the Illuminati. Kelly allegedly died in a vehicle accident after suffering a stroke. She was taken to the hospital, but on September 14, 1982, Rainier III instructed the physicians to turn off her life support a day after the tragedy. Kelly was seen to be no longer required and had to be sacrificed.

## Kurt Cobain was a rock and roll icon.

Despite his celebrity at the time, Cobain despised it. He said that all he wanted to do was share his songs. According to conspiracy theories, the Illuminati tried to put Cobain under mind control, but he rejected. As a result, the Illuminati plotted his demise. Even though his death was ruled a suicide, many conspiracy theories questioned the circumstances. Cobain died of a gunshot wound on April 5, 1994.

## Diana, Princess of Wales

Many conspiracy theorists think the Royal family plays an important role in the Order of the Illuminati. The divorce of Prince Charles and Princess Diana was a major source of shame for the Royals. Princess Di was no longer a royal family member, despite her fame and popularity in England and globally. As a result, she had to leave. Princess Di supposedly died in a vehicle accident on August 31, 1997. However, the inquest's ultimate judgment determined that her death was a murder rather than an accident.

## Michael Jackson is a well-known musician.

Many individuals believe Jackson was an Illuminati member. However, before his death, he started speaking out against the Order, claiming a plot to discredit him. As a result, he was dubbed a child molester and a weirdo. Michael's sister, La Toya Jackson, stated that her brother often mentioned a gang of people attempting to murder him. Jackson died in his bed on June 25, 2009, only days before his homecoming performance in London, from severe intoxication of propofol and benzodiazepine, which resulted in cardiac arrest. Later, his physician was found guilty of involuntary manslaughter.

## Celebrities Who Are Alleged Illuminati Members

The entertainment business is home to some of the world's most prominent and powerful individuals. Given that the Order of the Illuminati is a group of elite people, it's no surprise that they're drawn to the world of show business.

As described in earlier chapters, the Illuminati use symbols that may be meaningless to the average person. The symbol, however, is holy to the Order's members and may also indicate whether or not a person is a member. Other emblems besides the ones described before including goat heads, owls, and unicorns.

Members of the Illuminati are not regular people. They are the world's elite, and they include financial wizards, politicians, and celebrities. The following is a list of supposed Illuminati celebrities regarded as the best and most influential in their respective industries.

## Jay-Z is a well-known rapper.

He is not just a rapper but also regarded as the godfather of today's Illuminati. Those searching for evidence might look at how Jay-Z uses hand motions to display the Pyramid sign throughout his concerts and appearances. In several of his music videos, he has also used goat heads.

## Beyoncé's

When the husband is the leader in spreading the Illuminati's ideals, the wife naturally supports him. Beyoncé flashed the Illuminati symbol Pyramid in front of millions of living, online, and home viewers during the 2013 Super Bowl halftime concert. In addition, she modeled an outfit with a goat skull in a picture session. Blue Ivy, Jay-Z and Beyoncé's daughter, is said to be the Order's newest, if not the Order's youngest, member and might become another prominent personality in the future.

## Lindsay Lohan

It has been noted that Lohan flashes the triangle signal whenever she is photographed or undertakes a photoshoot. Her tattoo is a demonic red triangle with the words "What Dreams May Come." Many people feel she is blaming the Illuminati for assisting individuals in achieving celebrity.

## Lady Gaga

Lady Gaga, like Jay-Z and Beyoncé, has used goat heads in her music videos. She has also used unicorns and triangle iconography on her album covers and videos, indicating the Illuminati's flawless inception. Lady Gaga confessed to having a dream in which Lindsay Lohan rode a goat to the mountain of pyramids to meet the Lizard Queen, none other than Lady Gaga. As a result of this dream, she has performed an Illuminati ritual in many concerts.

## Rihanna's

Given that Jay-Z is her mentor and she is his protégé, it's no surprise that Rihanna is an Illuminati member. She doesn't shy away from showing it throughout her performances. Rihanna is often seen flashing the Pyramid sign with her hands. In her S&M video, she even displayed the title "Princess of the Illuminati." Riri was also claimed to be Rihanna in a tale about a remote Mexican goat farm.

## Madonna

Madonna incorporated a people pyramid and put horns on her helmet for her Super Bowl halftime show in 2012. It's also worth noting that two supposed Illuminati members, Beyoncé and Madonna, headlined the halftime performance two years ago. It might be a coincidence, but it's also plausible that the NFL is connected to the Illuminati.

## Kanye West

It is true that Jay-Z and Kanye West are excellent friends and that they are also professionally close. As a result, Kanye is almost certainly a member of the Illuminati. Kanye usually wears jewelry with Order symbols on it. In his music videos, he frequently incorporates supernatural themes.

## Celine Dion

According to legend, Celine's music is the work of the devil. This comes after she flashed Illuminati insignia while performing and showing the El Diablo or Devil's Horns sign. Although she is not as well-known as Jay-Z, Beyoncé, Lady Gaga, Rihanna, and other music superstars, she is known to recruit or mingle with other showbiz heavyweights. Some claim that her eyes are physically formed like the number 6, a favorite of Illuminati members.

## Justin Bieber

Bieber has been accused of being a member of the Illuminati Order since he donned clothes with pentagrams and flashed the A-Ok sign. Although many people think he's merely A-Ok, others believe there's more to him than his pentagram-printed shirts and flashing A-Ok. He, like Rihanna, is a fan of goat farms.

## Emma Watson

She was pictured with the number 6 framing her eye. That piece of evidence raised the possibility that she is a member of the Illuminati. Many people couldn't believe how beautiful she is, how she had such wonderful hair, how she completed her college degree despite her hectic schedules, and how she delivered her feminist speech at the United Nations. These folks believe that everything is the work of the Illuminati.

## Angelina Jolie

Her film selections, wild personal life, and donning a vial of Brad Pitt's blood are all very Illuminati. These are some of the reasons why many people assume Jolie is a member of the shadow organization. In addition to this, she has posed with a demonic hand motion. Several of her films, particularly the Tomb Raider trilogy, include elements of the all-seeing eye symbol.

## Paris Hilton

Hilton is reported to have been taught the methods of the Order of the Illuminati from a young age. Her family is obscenely affluent. Her music videos also use Order symbols. She uses the Shh hand sign not just in her pictures but also in her guest appearances. Many people think it is a salute to the Illuminati; if not, she may have been brainwashed by the secret organization.

## Chris Brown

Despite being the ex-boyfriend of Rihanna, another supposed Illuminati member, Brown has revealed himself as a member of the secret organization via his tattoos. One of them is a snake with a crimson pyramid at the tip of its tail and an eye in the center. He nearly usually performs half-naked or tank tops to give credit to the Illuminati through his back tattoo.

## Dr. Dre

People think he is a member of the Illuminati because of his best-selling Beats by Dre headphones and his relationships with some celebrities on this list. His headphones may be seen in many of the music videos of other supposed Illuminati celebs. In reality, these celebrities have heavily marketed Dre's headphones. Beats' anagram is Beast, implying his association with the shadow organization.

## Sean Combs

His riches and prominence in the music business are only a few signs of his Illuminati ties. However, he proved his participation in the shadow organization by flashing satanic hand motions and the Pyramid sign. Given his clout, his presence will be immensely beneficial to the Illuminati once the New World Order is established.

# CONCLUSION

I hope you enjoyed this book and learned more about the Illuminati!

The tale of the Illuminati Order is disclosed or suppressed, exposed, embellished, or mocked several times depending on the writers' and critics' points of view. Given the group's secrecy, obtaining the facts about the Illuminati may be very difficult. Throughout the years, several interpretations of the Illuminati's narrative have evolved. Some may be true, while others are purely fictitious. As previously said, it all relies on the author and reviewers and the audience to which they appeal.

While it is impossible to answer all concerns regarding the Illuminati, this book attempted to provide a fuller image of the Order, its aims and purposes, the makeup of its members, and current information about the secret organization.

Much of the material supplied is merely people's theories. It is up to you to determine what to believe and who you feel is a member of this nefarious organization.

Thank you, and best wishes!